HUNTERS

THE LARGEST ARMY IN THE WORLD
70 MILLION STRONG

Contributors Representing Over 550 Years of Hunting Experience!

Camo Don Dupart
Randy Malcore
Chris McDaniel
Doug Moorhead
Mark Porter
Scott Porter
Jim Panetti
Jamie Parker
Carl Parks
Mark Sisel
Jeff Thommes
Craig Whitt
Craig Zeise

First Printing: August 2023

Disclaimer: The information in this book is meant to supplement, not replace, proper hunting training.

ISBN: 979-8-218-23073-9

Printed by Kingery Printing,
Effingham, Illinois, United States of America

Jim Panetti, Collaborator

Contributors:
Camo Don Dupart
Randy Malcore
Chris McDaniel
Doug Moorhead
Jim Panetti
Mark Porter
Scott Porter
Jamie Parker
Carl Parks
Mark Sisel
Jeff Thommes
Craig Whitt
Craig Zeise

Layout by Kaylee Kelso (KayKelso, LLC | kaykelso.com)

Scripture is from the New Kings James Version, the New American Standard Bible 95, and the New International Version.

For information contact: https://TrophiesOfGrace.org

HUNTERS

Table of Contents

ENDORSEMENTS

While serving as a hunting guide for over 35 years across North America meeting thousands of sportsmen and sportswomen, I have read countless hunting books. From this experience and education, and having hunted and served with many of the hunters that contributed to this book, I know that these tips will guide outdoorsmen and women in the right direction. For example, you will learn about how to deal with the whitetail deer's eye sight, hearing, and sense of smell, as well as other enlightening hunting advice.

Every one of us is on the hunt for something in life including seeking out truth. This book intertwines hunting tips with some life-guidance essentials to help the reader be successful in their quest for both game and truth.

Dean Hulce

President and Host of God's Great Outdoors Radio and Trail to Adventure Podcasts Hunting and Fishing Guide

Past President of National Wild Turkey Federation and Safari Club International Chapters

Evangelist

I've been blessed to serve on the Trophies Of Grace Ministries Board of Directors, the publishing organization of this pocket reference guide. In addition, I have had the honor to hunt with many of the men that are part of this book and count them as close friends.

For over 40 years, I've guided hunters all across the western mountains of Alaska, South Dakota, and Colorado, and in the states of Michigan and Wisconsin. Countless times, I have been asked for hunting advice, especially regarding hunting elk, mule deer, and whitetails. If you are one of those looking for good hunting tips, you will find them in this book. And along the way, you will also discover vital tips for guiding your life.

Dave Hulce

Western Mountain Guide Specialist

Trophies of Grace Board Member

Director of High Impact Outdoors

David Carillet

Forward

Bringing over 550 years of hunting experience and 1,900 sporting events, wild game dinners, and barn meetings to the table, these hunters have learned a thing or two! Like other hunters, the authors of this pocket reference manual realize that even when listening to professional speakers of the highest caliber, wise discernment must be employed because not all advice is trustworthy. In the hunting arena, *hearing* expert advice and *experiencing* it sometimes yields different conclusions.

Hence, within its pages, this little book offers knowledge and skills these men wish they would have learned sooner, some that could have saved people a lot of unnecessary pain, and sometimes, someone's life.

Their combined experience harvesting many big game animals, including whitetails, red stag, elk, mule deer, antelope, bear, turkeys, gators, wild hogs, geese, moose, pythons, and rattlesnakes, place them at a level equal to that of a professional gun or bow hunting guide. No brag, just fact: thousands of hunting education hours in the wild qualify all these contributing hunters to aid you in a successful hunt.

Hunting is not for the faint-hearted, and let's face it: hunters incur injuries. But whether you are a hunter or not, our human bodies encounter the need for healing. We are broken. Why is that?

God created a perfect world desiring an intimate relationship with mankind (Genesis 1:31). When Adam and Eve chose to disobey Him, their relationship with God was broken, and sin entered the world. Since Adam, all humanity has lived under that curse and has disobeyed God. So, though our Creator God created a perfect world, sin entered that ideal world, leaving us with disease, destruction, and death. Thankfully, God provided the way of salvation to save us from this doom, and one day He will provide paradise again. Until then, we can live with the knowledge of how we can best thrive and best hunt under sin's curse. We hope you enjoy these stories and the tips they provide, and we double deer dare you to live and hunt with truth and wisdom from our Master Guide, Jesus Christ!

Mark Porter,
Trophies of Grace

EcoPrint & Improvisor
Shutterstock

HUNTING TIP #1

Courage in the Face of Danger

Imagine being in the military and fighting in Iraq. I once met a man who served there and was shot through the back of his ear. He was awarded a Purple Heart. Later, he was knocked out by an exploding IED and survived the attack. Though this brave soldier certainly far more deserved a Purple Heart for getting knocked out by the IED than a bullet going through the back of his ear, he did not receive a second Purple Heart because he didn't bleed. Despite all the dangers brought his way, this American hero explained his story in such a casual, peaceful way, he made it seem like everyday life!

Three times, I also experienced some close calls with bullets buzzing past me. One time while goose hunting in the cattails, I plainly heard a shotgun's BBs sizzle past me. On another occasion, a neighbor boy was repeatedly shooting at a squirrel when suddenly, one of the bullets whooshed past my head. Then there was the time I was hunting deer when another hunter's bullet hit the frozen plowed field, ricocheting his projectile back up to our 18-foot high tree stand. I will never forget the sound of that could-have-been-deadly bullet whizzing past my ear.

Crazy how the Lord protects us! In Psalm 91: 9-12, we read of God's protection. *"If you say, 'The LORD is my refuge,' and you make the Most High your dwelling, no harm will overtake you, no disaster will come near your tent. For he will command his angels concerning you to guard you in all your ways; they will lift you up in their hands, so that you will not strike your foot against a stone." —NIV*

These close calls could have turned our Purple Heart Veteran or myself cowering away from ever facing challenges involving ammunition again. Instead, they have served as lessons to sharpen our skills for God's glory!

Hunting Tip #1 Summary:

Always respect your weaponry and that of others. Be willing to learn from other, more experienced hunters. Place your life in the hands of the Living God who offers His peace and protection to His children.

Michael Tatman
Dreamstime

HUNTING TIP #2

If You Breathe, You're Busted

A deer's sense of smell is 1,000 times stronger than a human's! Their nose will bust you every time. For that reason, hunters must take every precaution to cover their scent, even taking precautions about something like their breath.

Overall, the key is: just as bloodhounds smell your sweat and flaking skin particles, so do the deer. You don't want to sweat or leave a scent trail. Wear rubber boots and use a product to extinguish your scent. Look inside your long underwear; skin flakes are everywhere. This problem is yet another to solve if you do not want to be busted by the deer. Here are a few tips for preparing to cover your scent!

- Scrape your skin with a loofah brush or bristle brush, which prepares your skin for up to two to three days.
- Put your hunting clothes in evergreen or cedar boughs a week before your hunting trip.
- Avoid overheating by dressing in layers, both while riding in your vehicle and when you are walking to your stand. Adjust your clothing layers as needed to avoid sweating.
- Wear camo clothes that are tightly knit to keep the exposed skin flaking at a minimum.
- Use scent-free shampoo and body wash.
- Use scent-free deodorant.
- Wash all clothing with scent-free laundry soap and softener, including underclothes, washcloths, and towels.
- Treat your clothes using an ozone generator to deodorize them.

- Cover your scents by using acorn waffle scent bombs.

- Chew apples and pine branches to cover your breath.

- Swish coconut oil in your mouth as it cleans teeth and gives your mouth a fresh feeling covering your breath scent. Because it pulls toxins from your body, spit it out.

- Chew Gum-O-Flage to cover your breath scent.

- Stop breathing. ☺Impractical, but it's the fastest way out of your tree stand when you pass out.

- Use Nose Jammer, a vanilla extract that deer love.

- Wear a charcoal scent-lock suit to absorb scent. Reactivate its properties by heating it in a dryer on high.

- Apply EverCalm Stick Em Wax on your boots, your stand, and the tree branches you can reach from your stand. Rain and dew will not wash EverCalm off your boots.

- Build your stand in an evergreen tree to mask your scent.
- Acid reflux also produces a scent that may sometimes be reduced by taking apple cider vinegar.
- Using wintergreen essential oil can also cover your human scent well.
- Baking soda absorbs odors.
- Use an ozone generator in your deer stand.
- Eliminate excessive does as necessary, as the more noses there are, the more chances you'll get busted.
- If you get sprayed by a skunk, use baking soda and hydrogen peroxide to change the composition of the skunk oil, thus removing the smell.

Though a considerable number of products have come out to combat your scent, you still can't beat good "woodsmanship." You must stay downwind from the deer.

Hunting Tip #2 Summary:

If you don't want to alert the deer, take scent control seriously!

Luke Jernejcic
Unsplash

HUNTING TIP #3

Stealth Mode

Like their sense of smell, a deer's sense of hearing is also acute! Research done by Dr. Henry Heffner at the University of Toledo shows that deer can hear upwards of 54,000 hertz. In comparison, humans only hear up to 20,000 hertz — if they are lucky. You can make noises you may not even know you're making but which deer can hear as clear as a bell.

Whitetails have large pinnae (the external ear) on their head, that they can rotate like radar dishes in any direction to pinpoint the slightest noise. Translation: Deer can collect vibrational sound waves from any angle, making their hearing even more sensitive to any noise you make.

Some hunters suggest making natural noises as you go into your blind by busting branches, rubbing trees, and bending over when walking in, much like the noises other deer make. Because deer are inquisitive, your entry should sound like another deer.

Others say silence is key, even raking their path and clearing the way a week ahead of their hunt to avoid making any noise from their own footsteps. Many suggest walking in while it's dark, again to arrive in stealth mode, moving slowly, and taking your time.

When bow hunting for deer, you are attempting to beat a deer at its own game. Deer make a living staying alive and avoid being preyed upon. You must outwit and outflank them by silently sneaking through the woods to a place where you are perched high above the forest floor, waiting for an unsuspecting deer to step into range.

Your movements must be stealthy and silent. If a deer

sees you, you have lost the battle, as they will retreat into the thick brush from where they came. You may be forced to move to another ambush position and try again. When you finally arrow the target animal and stand over it, you will know the battle has been won!

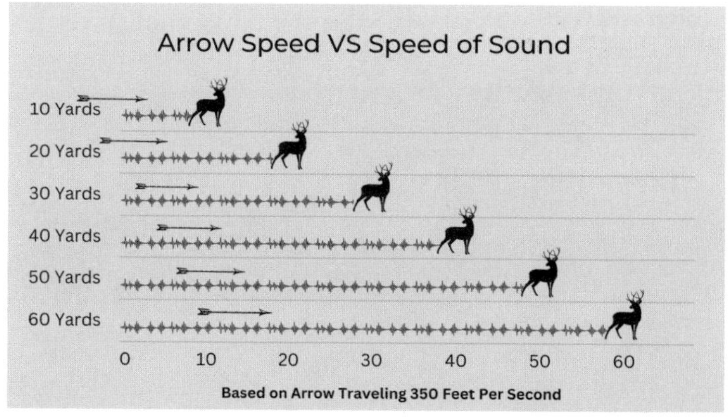

If you are a bowhunter, you may feel you've got your target once your arrow leaves your fingertips. Nope! Deer have been known to duck an arrow! When they ***hear*** the bow shot, they immediately start running, always squatting as they start. Then if they have time to ***see*** the arrow coming toward them, they jump it! The chart above demonstrates the arrow speed vs. the speed of sound.

Deer can hear the sound of a branch breaking from 400 yards away and the sound of your metal climbing stick clanging for one-half mile. That is why hunters must eliminate non-nature sounds such as metal clanging, a cell phone beeping or ringing, or a plastic bucket clunking. Even small things like a trail camera door closing can end the hunt.

Hunting Tip #3 Summary:

Because deer possess such superior hearing, if you want a successful hunt, think stealth mode!

Lassedesignen
Shutterstock

HUNTING TIP #4

Glowing in the Stand

Animals have specially designed eyesight. Deer see in blue and yellow colors. In nocturnal animals, a mirror-like layer of tissue called the tapetum bounces light back through the retina. Have you ever noticed an animal's eyes? They glow in the headlights, but human eyes don't.

Have you ever used the UV detector trick? That is when you put your camo clothes, including your hat, under a UV black light to see if they glow. If they do, you're a lightning bug in the woods. That is what the deer see. You must get rid of that glow!

You can stop your hunting clothes from glowing, but it often takes 40 washings to get out the brighteners that many detergents contain that cause that glow. You can also use a UV Killer Spray on your clothes before washing them to break the chain of the glowing fibers to ward off your luminosity.

Another tactic to keep the deer from spotting you is to use a blind. This helps hide both your scent and movement. Your chances for success increase incredibly in a box blind.

HECS Technology is another tool for stopping a different glow, your electrical glow. Muscle movements and even your beating heart produce electrical energy which is emitted from our bodies. Animals are capable of detecting these electrical energy emissions. Clothing with HECS technology blocks your electrical signature, making you less detectable by animals, stopping them from sensing your electrical glow.

A buck on high alert has three defense mechanisms: scent, sound, and sight. If a buck senses even one warning, they flee!

Hunting Tip #4 Summary:

You may want a glowing personality, but you don't want any glow in your deer stand!

Vincent Van Zalinge
Unsplash

HUNTING TIP #5

The Great Debate

After you shoot, **when** do you recover your animal? In hunting, to go or to wait, THAT is the question. The great debate then is whether to retrieve your game right away while the buck is stunned, or to keep your eye and gun on the spot where the buck fell and wait. Many hunters choose to let the buck bleed out. However, you risk the buck reviving and running away. *(Your shot placement significantly affects whether an animal is stunned, wounded, or killed. See Tip #8, Optics and Shot Placement.)*

Part of analyzing this question requires understanding your firearm and the ammunition's effect on an animal. A hunter needs a bullet with a minimum of 1000- foot-pound velocity to hunt deer. Therefore, knowing the *appropriate* power of your ammunition and rifle is paramount. If you use too light of velocity ammunition, you may only wound the animal.

For example, the 30-06 releases at a velocity of 3250 foot pounds, which is 20 times stronger than a 308 rifle cartridge. The 7mm and 300 mag is 50 times more powerful than the 30-06. Velocities of at least 2500 foot pounds are helpful in stunning a deer for ten seconds to sometimes an hour before they get up.

If you are bow hunting, you also must evaluate the best arrow to use on your hunt. A fixed blade produces a smaller entry and exit hole, while a mechanical, expandable blade can cause up to a three-inch cut. The disadvantage of an expandable arrow is that it slows the arrow down, not allowing it to penetrate the animal deep enough to kill it. While a hunter may make a perfect shot at 15 yards with a 70-pound bow, the 3-inch expandable blade may only penetrate about 4 inches. Thus, that buck will be recovered days later when the birds lead you to him.

Ultimately the great debate is whether to retrieve your game while he is stunned before he revives and runs away, or to wait, hoping he will bleed out. If the deer revives and runs, you have the terrible situation of a wounded, suffering animal full of adrenaline that spoils the venison.

Hunting Tip #5 Summary:

Galatians 6:9 says, *"Let us not become weary in doing good, for at the proper time we will reap a harvest if we do not give up."* —NIV

Huseyin Bostanci
iStock

HUNTING TIP #6

Your Guide

When hunting, you need guides. Your earthly hunting guide offers much to those who will listen. He has knowledge from years of hunting experience. He pays attention to obvious signs like deer runways and droppings, as well as not-so-obvious signs like broken branches and rubs. A good guide is aware of when the deer are feeding (about every four to five hours) and what affects their eating patterns. For example, when the barometer drops just before a storm, the animals, fish, and birds go into a feeding frenzy. When the moon is up night or day, this also brings the wildlife out to feed.

A great earthly guide will provide a shooting stick that

helps you with your shot placement. He knows the deer patterns of the area and helps with baiting techniques where legal. He provides game camera footage that alerts you to the animals in the area. And most of all, your guide must be trustworthy! The following true story by Hunter Scott Porter demonstrates this point all too well.

In the fall of 2002, I found myself in the deep woods of Ontario, Canada stalking a beautiful black bear. The guide and I had located him feasting on wild blueberries about ¾ of a mile away at the edge of a large cutover. The wind was perfect, so off we went. Keeping our eyes on him, we were able to maneuver closer and closer without being detected. After about an hour of pursuit, we had to go through a deep ravine which meant we would lose sight of him temporarily until we climbed up to the other side.

Taking it slowly so as not to make any noise, we worked our way through and up the other side of the ravine. Carefully, we began emerging out of our cover with hardly any movement because we knew the bear was close. Wow! He was basically on top of us! There he stood, not 20 yards in front of me. Slowly, I raised my rifle and fired. What a hunt! The guide and I "high-fived" each other, and I excitedly proclaimed that it was probably the most exhilarating hunt I had ever experienced.

Now, the real work began. After a long evening of packing the bear out of the woods, I relaxed with the other two hunters who had joined me on the hunt. By the end of the week, the other two hunters had harvested their bears, and we began our trip back to Florida. What a great hunt we all had; so pleased with the licensed outfitter located deep in the woods above Thunder Bay, Ontario, that had been guiding big game and fishing expeditions for over 40 years.

Fast forward three years to May of 2005. I was working at my real estate office when the receptionist told me that two US Fish and Wildlife Officers would like to speak with me. I greeted them, and we all went to the conference room where they explained they wanted to ask some questions about the bear hunt I had been on three years earlier. Being an avid hunter my entire life, I knew this meant there was a problem. After all, local game wardens and US Fish and Wildlife Service never show up at your doorstep years later to congratulate you on a great hunt!

I sat down with the two officers, and they asked numerous questions about the bear hunt for over an hour. Since I had nothing to hide, I shared all the details I knew including that I had taken my skin to a taxidermist to be made into a bear rug. When they concluded the interview, they informed me that they needed to confiscate the bear rug because I had killed the bear *illegally*.

"Illegally!" I blurted out. "What do you mean I killed the bear illegally? I purchased a bear tag from the outfitter and tagged the bear. I purchased the required habitat stamp and nonresident license, and I declared the bear at the border with US Customs!" Later, I even provided them all the legal paperwork I had secured before ever hunting in Canada, proving I had done nothing wrong.

They understood I had done nothing wrong but then explained that my guide had put me out to hunt on land for which he did not have bear rights. That meant that any bear killed on that land was harvested illegally. They further informed me that I was facing *felony charges* related to the Lacey Act for illegally bringing the bear across state lines! I was in shock, to say the least!

The federal officers followed me to my house and confiscated my bear rug right off the wall. What a disaster! With attorneys and thousands of dollars defending myself, the US Fish and Wildlife Service ended up dropping all charges. Still, they would not return the bear rug because it was harvested on land for which the outfitter did not have hunting rights. *I had put my trust in the wrong guide!*

Years have passed since that incident. While reflecting on the course of events of that hunt, a jolting thought came to me, "How many people put their trust in the wrong guide to get them to heaven?" When I went on that bear hunt, I was very sincere about making sure I did everything right in the law's eyes. I had researched outfitters, bought a license, a habitat stamp, and a CITES tag, and declared the bear at the border. I had done everything right except for one thing; I chose the wrong guide in whom to place my trust.

When it comes to your spiritual journey, who are you putting your trust in for guidance? My hope is that you will put your trust in Jesus Christ alone. God is extremely clear in his Word that doing good does not save you. God is also emphatic that there is no other way to heaven except through His Son, Jesus Christ. The Bible, God's Word, says in John 14:6, *"Jesus said to him, "I am the way, the truth, and the life. No one comes to the Father except through Me."* —NKJV

We all need guides in our lives who we can trust. Our Heavenly Father can guide you physically and spiritually. Though we make poor choices sometimes, God is never wrong. That's why it is so important to choose God as your Heavenly Father and your Number One Guide. Deuteronomy 1:13 *"Choose wise, understanding, and knowledgeable men from among your tribes, and I will make them heads [guides] over you."* Proverbs 19:20-21 says *"Listen to counsel and accept discipline, that you may be wise the rest of your days. Many plans are in a man's heart,* ***but the counsel of the LORD will stand.****"* —NKJV

Perhaps you have no relationship with the Creator of the Universe. You can! It is as simple as A, B, C.

1. Admit you are a sinner. (Romans 3:10; 3:23; 6:23)
2. Believe that Jesus' death, burial, and resurrection is the only perfect, acceptable payment for your sin. (Romans 5:8-9)
3. Confess you are a sinner to God the Father and ask Him to forgive you because of the finished work of Jesus. (Romans 10:9-10, 13)

You can talk to the Heavenly Guide just like you can talk to an earthly guide. We call that praying. Though there are no magic prayers to get anyone to Heaven or establish a relationship with God, this simple prayer tells you what you could pray from your heart.

Dear God,

I believe that Jesus died for my sins, was buried, and rose on the third day. I admit that because of my sin, I need the redemption that is offered through Your Son's sacrifice, and I receive it with a grateful heart.

From this moment on, I want to follow You. Until you call me home to Heaven, help me to live in a relationship looking forward to spending eternity in Heaven with You forever. Thank You for accepting me into Your family.

In Christ's mighty name I pray, Amen.

Hunting Tip #6 Summary:
Put your trust in those who are trust-worthy, both for your earthly guide, and even more importantly, your Heavenly Guide!

leonard78uk
iStock

HUNTING TIP #7

Lucky Buck or *Unlucky* Buck?

You are hunting. So, how can you attract deer? Many items fall into the category of a deer's appetite.

One of those items is an all-time favorite of many humans, too. Peanut Butter! A simple way to use this tip is to unscrew the lid of a peanut butter jar and nail it to a tree. Next screw the peanut butter jar back onto the lid and cut off the bottom of the jar. Instant treat accessibility for the deer!

Another scent deer love is vanilla. Nose Jammer, a vanilla-smelling spray, not only attracts the deer, but also covers your human scent. It's a win—win.

Deer need minerals for a variety of health reasons. The newborns need them for building strong bones, and mature bucks need them to grow big antlers. Thus many hunters help provide this needed nutrient for the deer population.

Products like Lucky Buck or Antler King provide these needed minerals. For optimum results, these minerals must be placed out in the woods before your first lawn mowing. Deer thrive on minerals in the spring but won't as readily eat them in the fall. That's why the spring season is when you should use these products.

In the spring, prepare a 6-foot x 6-foot plot by softly raking the ground and spreading the minerals there. In the fall, switch to acorn wafers or molasses if you want to keep the deer coming back.

Caution: Some states have hunting laws prohibiting baiting and mineral licks. Be sure you know the laws in the area you are hunting.

Hunting Tip #7 Summary:

Healthy deer, happy hunters.

Joe Cox
Unsplash

HUNTING TIP #8

Optics and Shot Placements

One of the most critical elements to understand when hunting is shot placement and optics. Knowing you can place that shot wherever you need to is essential. Therefore, hunters need a good quality scope for the most economical price.

Then practice with that scope. A great way to start is to have a statue of an elk or a deer that can be moved easily. You will need to practice with the target turned to different positions.

Never shoot at a 60-degree angle with a bow because the arrow will glance off the rib cage. This injures the animal instead of killing it. Always look for broadside shots behind the front leg, not quartering away shots, as a broadside shot will take out both lungs or the heart, making it a quick kill. There is nothing worse than a wounded buck, turkey, or duck. The adrenalin goes into the meat producing a "wild taste." Guys like to make it more of a challenge by downgrading to a pistol or recurve bow, but let's kill the animal quickly rather than making it suffer.

Have a camera on your scope or a guide to record your hunt. After the shot, you can then see whether the shot is good or bad. Scopes come in 32, 40, and 50 bell sizes. The 50 bell gives you a much wider view of moving animals. Put your scope ahead of the animal. When he enters the field of vision, pull the trigger using the tip of your finger.

Tips for accurate shot placement:

- Make sure your scope is dialed down from your target practice.

- Compare the speed of sound to the speed of the arrow.
- Make sure you purchase a rangefinder and scope with bold letters.
- Know that a muzzleloader may discharge 2 seconds after you pull the trigger.

Hunting Tip #8 Summary:

If you want a successful hunt in the most merciful way, KNOW your shot!

JOB, MONEY, WIVES, AND LOTS OF SLEEP

HAVE BEEN LOST OVER THIS ADDICTION

Sebastian Pociecha & Federico Di Dio Photography
Unsplash

HUNTING TIP #9

Addictions

Addiction: *the state of being compulsively committed to a habit or practice or to something that is psychologically or physically habit-forming to such an extent that its cessation causes an unhealthy dependence, changing proper moral obligations and priorities.*

Addictions come in many forms, some you may not think of as addictions: drugs, pornography, sports, television, alcohol, gambling, cell phones, computers, food, fishing, hunting, and more. But regardless of what you battle that controls your life, it comes down to a choice. Sadly, many people won't pay for their health needs like dental care, proper exercise, and medical conditions, spending their money on their "addictions" instead.

Perhaps you can't imagine hunting becoming an addiction, but stealing away to the solitude of the woods can become your drug of choice. That may not be a problem at first. However, it can become your personal adrenaline, your escape from your duties as an employee, husband, father, or son, or even your relationship with the Creator who designed the entire universe for your pleasure.

Maybe you can relate to one hunter's story. The night before their big hunt, booked months in advance, this hunter's wife went into labor. Now, where do you think that hunter wanted to be: at the hospital by his wife's side giving birth to their firstborn child or with the hunting group in a deer stand? You guessed it. The deer stand. Maybe it had become an addiction, one that skewed his priorities.

Addictions often come slowly, almost without recognition by the abuser. In one way or another, you become possessed—sometimes even demon-possessed.

But there is hope and a process for healing. We can call on the name of Jesus by the authority of the Word of Jesus' testimony and the blood of the Lamb to help us overcome addictions and demon possession. Many Christian counselors are available to help those who want to experience freedom. Take advantage of their experience and seasoned wisdom. Some excellent resources include: *Defeated Enemies* by Corrie ten Boom, *Spiritual Warfare* by Dr. Karl Payne, and *How to Defeat Harmful Habits* by June Hunt.

Addictions bring horrible consequences to our lives and the ones we love. If you are struggling with an addiction, even a hunting one, please get help because you cannot carry the weight of an addiction alone.

Hunting Tip #9 Summary:

If something in your life has become an escape from your responsibilities, reevaluate whether it has become an unhealthy addiction. God can give you victory over it. Matthew 6:33 *"But seek first the kingdom of God and His righteousness, and all these things will be added to you."* —NKJV

Hari Nandakumar
Unsplash

HUNTING TIP #10

Preparing for the Battle

In preparation for the hunt, make your checklist. You'll be glad you did. Many hunters made blunders, such as mixing up ammunition, forgetting their range finder, failing to replace the battery in their range finder, or not taking the time to check the wind direction. All these preparations and more are so important. Making a checklist may seem like a waste of your time. In reality, it will save you both time and frustration.

Here are a few items for your checklist:

- Gun and bullets

- Bow, arrows, bow rope, and release
- Harness for the tree stand
- Knife
- Binoculars
- Flashlight
- Thermacell to fight the mosquitos
- Thermos
- Rope
- Lighter
- Reading glasses
- Odor free seat cushion
- Spare cell battery for your bow sight
- Regarding your calls: Hang your rattling horns on a rope with the rattling horns at the ground level so as not to disclose your position.

- Snort-Wheeze Call - This brings in the dominant buck and scares away smaller bucks. (If you are a small buck shooter, buy all your hunter friends a snort-wheeze call to scare all the smaller bucks over to you!)

- Grunt Call - Start with a lower volume; if there is no response, gradually increase the volume in 2 or 3 different directions.

- Doe Bleat - This puts deer at ease where they do not sense danger.

- Rattle Bag or Rattling Antlers - Use light rattling in pre-rut; during the rut, make the sequence much louder, like the bucks are really fighting.

⦿ Gas up the day before, especially if using diesel fuel.

⦿ Put your phone on silent.

⦿ Use your rangefinder and know your ranges.

When buying a rangefinder or scope, buy one with bold letters.

- Don't overload; carry essential items of food and drink.
- Make sure your scope is dialed down from target practice.
- Bring a cloth to defog your scope in early mornings or freezing weather.
- Make sure your hot seat is odor free.
- Wear noiseless, layered clothing.
- Consider adding hand warmers, foot warmers, and heated jackets in cold weather.
- A rain-drenched forest provides an excellent surface for quiet stalking.
- Bring toilet paper to mark a blood trail.

Hunting Tip #10 Summary:

Pack light, but pack the essentials!

Luke 22:36 *"And He said to them, "But now, whoever has a money belt is to take it along, likewise also a bag, and whoever has no sword is to sell his coat and buy one." —NASB95*

"The treasure which you think not worth taking the trouble and pains to find, this one alone is the real treasure you're longing for all your life."
(B. Traven, *The Treasure of the Sierra Madre.)*
Chimperil59
iStock

HUNTING TIP #11

Turkey Tales and Other Drivel

Turkey Tale #1

Dawn. My father and I had made our way to our blind on the edge of the woods. The hardwoods were cold, vaporous, and wet. Dad was older now, and I always wanted to make our time together turkey hunting extra special. Little did I know that this hunt would be our last together, as Alzheimer's would claim Dad just a year and a half later.

The first throaty gobble came at 5:15am, and we both reacted with a toothy smile! I held fast to my rule of not calling right after a gobble, but instead, I flapped my hat against my leg to sound like a turkey flying down off its roost. This brought gobbles from every direction as the woods burst alive. By now, a mere 3/4 of an hour into the hunt, the mist had burned off, and the sun penetrated the hardwoods in shafts of cathedral light.

Dad did, in fact, bag a gobbler that day! Its fan and beard hang in my living room, along with a picture of Dad and me with his trophy. Many times since that hunt, hiking back to the pickup truck under faint starlight, I wonder what it is I've done right in my life to deserve such a gift.

Turkey Tale #2

Two hunters and a guide hunting turkey set out their decoy and went to sit by a massive oak tree to disguise their silhouette. Out of the corner of their eyes, they saw a fox running toward the decoy. However, it changed its path to attack the turkey decoy from the rear. Suddenly, only ten feet from the turkey decoy, the fox froze. Though the fox never saw the hunters, he had caught a whiff of their scent. Blasting out 30 yards, the fox strangely stopped again. He turned to look back at the decoy. Then totally confused, he ran away. Those hunters' camo gear must have been perfect that day!

Turkey Tale #3

There is nothing more magical than slipping into the woods on an early spring morning and watching God's beautiful creation come alive. Sitting in anticipation of the first gobble from a mature longbeard makes that morning even more special. As the woods become active with all God's creation, and the longbeard responds with a gobble to the hunter's call, the expectation builds with the turkey getting closer and closer. The bright red head finally appears from the direction you have been anxiously focused upon. It is the moment you have waited for all morning.

You slowly raise your gun in anticipation of finally making the last call before pulling the trigger. As you stare down the end of your barrel and line up the shot, out of nowhere the longbeard becomes spooked and begins clucking. Thoughts start racing through your mind. "How did the longbeard bust me?"

Out of nowhere, you catch a glimpse of something running towards the longbeard, which instantly takes off running and takes flight for cover. All at once, you realize that it was not you who spooked the longbeard, but a coyote, one of the wild turkey's worst predators. You know that your hunt is over. The question arises in your mind if the morning is wasted. You were so close to finishing the hunt by pulling the trigger. But then you remember the passage of scripture that states the following. *"Rejoice always, pray continually, give thanks in all circumstances; for this is God's will for you in Christ Jesus."* 1 Thessalonians 5:16-18

So no matter what circumstances life may throw at you, be thankful that God blessed you with a beautiful sunrise where you got to see the woods come alive! But don't forget, that thunder chicken's pea-sized brain won again!

Hunting Tip #11 Summary:

No matter what circumstances your hunt or your life brings, remember that God *blessed you* with another day of life.

HUNTING TIP #12

Rubs, Mock Scrapes, and Tracks

When searching out a good place for a deer stand, look for heavy deer runways, rubs, dropping, and scraps! These are important because you know bucks are close by. Every one to two days, a buck returns to check his scrape!

Mock Scrapes, when done properly, provide the hunter with his most lethal weapon for success. If you can't bait, design the perfect mock scrape. You can find many designs online.

Here are a few attributes to include in a quality mockscrape:

- Use only one licking branch or vine at each stand location.
- Use only deer urine in the scrape. (Men sure complain about high gas prices but have no problem paying $1,850 per gallon for deer urine!)
- Place deer urine in a bottle with cotton poked in the top of the bottle and hang it in a tree, or incorporate the heat wave urine technique. (See HeatWaveHunting.com).
- Place a licking branch chest height.
- Use a 3/4 to 1-inch diameter vine and tie it to a tree branch.
- Use a natural vine rather than rope, as natural is always better.
- Make an ideal licking branch with a length of about 6 feet and a curve.
- Remember that bucks rub the velvet off their antlers from approximately September 4—10.

- Be aware that there are three ruts until all of the does are bred.

- Hunt during the main rut, which usually runs October 31 to November 14. Check your local hunting club for exact dates in your area.

Hunting Tip #12 Summary:

To improve your hunt, go during the main rut and employ mock scrapes. These elements considerably increase your odds for success!

Bonita R. Cheshier
Shutterstock

HUNTING TIP #13

Field Care of Your Animal

Every whitetail hunter's ultimate goal is to harvest a trophy of a lifetime, and the hunt starts well before the season begins. After all the planning, strategizing, and anticipating, the day finally arrives when we can stand over our harvest in amazement. What an incredible feeling that is! But after recovering your buck, what's next? One avid hunter said, "The best way to mess up a deer hunt is to kill something." Obviously, he was being facetious, but he was correct that planning for this part of the hunt in advance is just as important as the other preliminary steps. Here are some hints:

1. Tag your animal.

2. Picture time! Prior to taking photographs, clean any blood off of the nose and mouth area. Also, if his tongue is hanging out, push it back into his mouth. Fold his front legs up under his belly. Smile!

3. The next thing you need to do is field dress it and get it cool. You must cool the carcass as soon as possible. Don't cut up past the sternum, and follow a diagram for field dressing a buck for the taxidermy if you plan to keep it for a mount.

4. Do your homework to find a quality taxidermist in your area. Don't skimp on the cost of mounting your buck of a lifetime.

5. If possible, avoid dragging your trophy for long periods, as it can damage the shoulder hair.

6. Beginning on the underside of the deer, slit the outer skin of the abdomen from the center of the rib cage to the groin area with a shallow incision being careful not to penetrate the membrane that

separates the hide from the stomach.

7. Cut around the scrotum on both sides and remove the testicles from the carcass.
8. Pull out the stomach, the liver, lungs, and heart.
9. Cut off the esophagus in the neck area.
10. Work on the bottom half of the carcass, slitting around the rectum.
11. Be cautious not to puncture the bladder.
12. Wrap a string around the bladder and cut it loose.
13. Take the rectum out of the back of the carcass.
14. Never hang your buck from its neck.
15. Flip the buck over to drain the blood.
16. Don't drive around in warm temperatures for long periods, as the warm temps can allow bacteria to grow, causing hair slippage.

Hunting Tip #13 Summary:

If you want a beautiful mount and good meat, planning and executing proper field care of your animal is vital.

"The new guy has a slight fear of bugs."

HUNTUNG TIP #14

Beating the Bugs

Did you know that deet and other chemical sprays are poisonous to humans as well as the bugs? Though not enough to kill us like it kills the bugs, these insect repellents seriously damage our bodies, especially children's little bodies. These sprays are quickly absorbed through our skin, our largest organ, and enter our bloodstream in less than a minute. **So if you use these chemical repellents, only spray them on clothing to prevent skin absorption.**

Hunters usually prefer their Thermacells. These units are the best defense weapon to keep pesky mosquitoes away. The fuel-powered Thermacell technology uses heat-activated repellent to create an invisible, scent-free zone of protection from mosquitoes. The active ingredient is Allethrin, a synthetic version of a naturally occurring repellent found in chrysanthemum flowers.

Hints for beating the bugs:

- Know how to replace the Thermacell pad and fuel cartridge.
- Use essential oils like lemongrass, eucalyptus, clove, citronella, or others to repel the pests.
- Keep wood ticks off by using double-sided tape around your ankles and calves.
- Put Stick-Em on a blue cup, as deer and horse flies love the color blue, and this will limit their choice of landing on you, making them stick to the cup instead.
- Make sure you are taking vitamins and minerals, because bugs tend to attack you more if you are low on these.

- Drink Ninja or Xango juice.
- Use MaxForce Fly bait.
- Use a bug assault gun.
- Employ oxygen therapy.
- Remember that bugs hate garlic.
- Apply Permethrin to your clothing, not your skin, to repel many pesky bugs including: flies, mosquitos, fleas, cockroaches, and ticks.
- Utilize an Ozone Generator in your stand to kill fleas, ticks, cockroaches, flies, and mosquitoes.

Hunting Tip #14 Summary:

If the bugs are bothering you, making you wave your arms around, your success rate buzzes right down the tube!

Randy Malcore

HUNTING TIP #15

Stand Placement

There are two types of hunters: those that have fallen out of a tree stand and those who will!

By now, you may be reconsidering hunting altogether or rethinking if it is possible to overcome all these challenges to actually get a buck. But if you watch big bucks, they will teach you. Proverbs 25:2 says, *"It is the glory of God to conceal a matter, But the glory of kings is to search out a matter." —NASB95*

God's Word encourages us to continue searching and learning. If you are still reading this book, then you are obviously doing just that. So here are tips regarding your tree stand. You may save yourself a heap of trouble by taking heed to them.

- After hunting season ends, walk the property to find the most-used trails, as they will be well-worn by this time.
- Use topical maps to identify knobs and pinch points (or funnels) to set up a stand.
- Use trail cams to discover the deer patterns.
- Do all of your stand work in the spring. Don't build stands in the fall, as this human intrusion during hunting season may cause the bucks to become nocturnal, ruining your chances of success.
- Try to set your stand in evergreens to help cover your scent.
- Deer love acorns, so an oak grove is a perfect choice for your stand.
- Look for heavy runways and a pinch point (or funnel) of buck travel.

- Find scrapes and buck rubs. All scrapes will have a licking branch that a buck will rub its glands on and a urine mark in the scrape. Bucks tend to check their scrapes every one to two days.
- Make mock scrapes with hanging branches or vines (see Tip #11).
- Add a box blind to your tree stand whenever possible to stop the buck or doe from seeing movement and spotting you. The box blind also helps block the wind from carrying your scent.
- Have a moveable stand for best wind placement or have several different stands from which to choose depending on the wind direction. You must stay downwind from the animal, or you will see the deer snort, stamp their leg on the ground, and warn every deer in the area of your spot.
- Look for droppings.
- Look for where bucks are feeding.

- Try to have multiple stands so if you are busted, you can move to another stand for the day.
- Put bait out a month before deer season begins, as a big buck won't come to a newly placed smell.
- The less you do to your stand close to deer season, the better your chances of getting your big buck.
- Absolutely do not disturb the bedding areas close to hunting season.
- To ensure the deer does not look up and see you, place your stand at least 233 feet in the air. ☺ Be sure to let us know if you find a 300-foot tree!☺

Hunting Tip #15 Summary:

As with selling a house, all that matters is location, location, location. Then add curb appeal to sweeten up your odds.

Camo Don

HUNTING TIP #16

Twenty Ways to Raise Your Recovery Odds

1. Have bright trail tracking equipment, such as a bright flashlight for tracking at night.

2. Make sure that you watch where the buck runs and listen for the sound of breaking branches.

3. Mark the spot where the buck was last seen with a hat, a tree limb, or tissue paper.

4. Check for blood, hair, arrow, and bone, and mark the animal's trail.

5. Walk *along* the blood trail, not *on* it.

6. Check the height of the blood trail if you're in tall grass.
7. Move slowly, watching carefully to see if the deer jumps up ahead of you.
8. Mark the last spot of blood.
9. Check the blood for bubbles or dark red spots.
10. Mark the point of loss very clearly.
11. Contact neighboring landowners.
12. Call a dog tracker, as advice is free.
13. Call a tracker before a grid search.
14. Find a group/map tracker for your state, such as IDTN, Illinois Deer Tracker's Network for the state of Illinois.
15. Employ the use of a drone, as the newest technology includes a spot light, GPS, and thermal and night vision cameras yielding hunters the sometimes-needed bonus of night vision

capability. (Contact Austin Carter of Carter Creek Drone Services at CarterCreekDroneServices@yahoo.com; 608-515-3681)

16. If you lose the blood trail, it's probably because the animal's fat has plugged the wound. At that point, it is time to call for a dog because you now have a wounded, suffering animal.

17. Look for a bed with blood in it because deer will lie down to recover.

18. If you have a questionable shot, back out and return the next day with a group of hunters to assist in locating the deer. This is necessary because if the deer is not dead, he will run, possibly to someone else's property.

19. If a deer has been shot in the stomach, his stomach acid goes into his bloodstream, and he will die within eight hours.

20. Pray. That is something we should all do first. But let the record state that many times when we

hunters have not been able to find a creature, then we pray, God miraculously directs our path to recover the animal.

By this time, you know that it's almost impossible to shoot a trophy buck and recover it, but keep your Spirits up; with God, all things are possible. You can also communicate with others who watch big bucks every day and learn from them "the ways of the great buck."

Hunting Tip #16 Summary:

Like humans, the older the buck, the more teeth they lose, the less they go for the females, and all their energy goes into just trying to survive!

Benjamin Lehman
Unsplash

HUNTING TIP #17

Deer Attractants

Tarsal Glands

Women wear perfume to attract men; men wear cologne to attract women. So, too, a deer's tarsal glands secrete an oily matter (sebum) that attracts other deer. The deer's tarsal glands are found on the inside of the rear hocks. Alone, the tarsal gland does not have much of an odor. But when a deer urinates on them and the urine decomposes, a scent unique to each individual deer becomes noticeable. Not only bucks, but even does and fawns rub-urinate year-round, with bucks doing this more often during the breeding season. Scientists speculate that tarsal glands provide whitetails with information on a deer's dominance status, sex, health.

Are tarsal glands effective for attracting deer? Like the answer to many questions, the answer is, "It depends." First, tarsal glands are most effective during the pre-rut when bucks are establishing their dominance. The scent of a young buck's tarsal glands may draw in an older, more dominant buck to see who is invading his territory. If you happen to harvest a dominant buck and use his tarsal glands as an attractant in the same area, it may scare off the dominant bucks. But using these same dominant buck's tarsal glands in a different location may bring the dominant buck in your new area out looking for the intruder.

Draglines

Tarsal glands can be removed from the deer and used as is, or broken down to use as a liquid scent. Caution! Bacteria in a deer's tarsal glands can cause illnesses in humans, so use rubber gloves when handling them. The tarsal glands can easily be removed by skinning around the gland and removing the entire gland. Store the glands in a ziplock bag and put them in the refrigerator or freezer.

When you are ready to use the tarsal gland, cut a small hole in the edge of it and tie a 6' paracord into the hole. Drag the gland behind you as you walk to your stand. Once at your stand, walk around it dragging the gland to create several areas where a buck would likely cross. Then hang the gland within shot distance of your stand where the wind will carry the scent in a cross-wind direction to the deer's anticipated direction.

Besides tarsal glands, you can also use EverCalm, Estrus doe scent, buck urine, and doe urine on your dragline. Apply these on a piece of cloth and attach it to a string on your belt, letting it drag behind you as you walk to your stand. These may cover your scent, calming the deer and making them feel safe.

Hunting Tip #17 Summary:

Making the deer feel comfortable in a natural-scented environment will help keep deer from being on high alert, improving your opportunities for a successful hunt.

Mark Kayser
markkayser.com

HUNTING TIP #18

Shed Hunting

Sometimes hunters use an alternate way of retrieving a "trophy" from nature. Shed Hunting involves finding the deer's antlers after they have been shed. You end up with a beautiful mount, even though you have not taken a shot. This is a different type of hunt, so it helps to know where to look. After all, who wants to look for a needle in a haystack, right?

First, bucks usually shed their antlers after all the doe have been bred when the ruts and hunting season are over. Then the deer herd up to survive against their predators during the winter when food is scarce. Thus, you want to look in their bedding grounds.

Second, look in the places where their feeding area is located, especially where their food source is most abundant. There will be heavy trails leading to these feeding grounds.

Third, fence crossings or tree lines can also be good places to look. When jumping a barbed wire fence, many horns are knocked off due to the jolt.

Finally, follow a good trail to a field and carefully check its wooded edge, as deer spend extra time there making sure it is safe to go out into the open field. The animals are often nervous and rub on brush and trees, knocking antlers off at the field's edge.

Hunting Tip #18 Summary:

If you want "trophy antlers" without taking a shot, look at the deer bedding grounds, fence lines, and food sources for their shed antlers!

Jeff Nissen
Unsplash
Exsodus
Dreamstime

HUNTING TIP #19

Communicating on Your Journey

Hunters love communicating with other hunters months before the hunt. They discuss what animal they want to get, looking at photos to help them plan. Then there is the hunt when you talk about what you see and wonder if any animals will come your way. You hear a shot, wonder who fired, and anxiously wait to see their picture of what they shot. What a story, and we hunters love stories!

When we think of hunting, we love looking at the prize, but the reward is really more about the journey, the story behind the trophy. That's what we love to listen to—someone's account describing the hunt's journey. So too, it is in life. What people really want to hear about is your progression, your story about your journey with Christ, your desire to be the man or woman that God has called you to be.

John Scott, an English clergyman and devotional writer in the early 1600s, wrote: "Life is a pilgrimage of learning, a voyage of discovery, in which our mistaken views are corrected, our distorted notions adjusted, our shallow opinions deepened, and some of our vast ignorances diminished." We hope this book of hunting tips has helped you adjust some of your hunting techniques and correct some mistaken ideas. But more than that, along the way, we hope you see the importance of communicating with earthly family and friends, and your eternal, loving Creator.

Yes, one day, we will rejoice and lay ourselves and our crowns at the feet of our Heavenly Guide. But He's interested in your relationship with Him along the way. God created us for fellowship with Himself and others.

Are you on a grand adventure to know God? Are you on the path that will allow you to tell Him an amazing story of how you overcame adversity, focused on the target, and made the shot?

If not, we would love to introduce you to the God of the universe, the One who will walk with you every step of your incredible journey!

Hunting Tip #19 Summary:

Be a good friend and communicator, sharing details to allow others 'to be in the tree' with you. Realize that recounting your story helps others along their own quest. And never forget that your journey and communication with the one and only Creator God remains paramount. Matthew 25:23 *"His lord said to him, 'Well done, good and faithful servant; you have been faithful over a few things, I will make you ruler over many things. Enter into the joy of your lord.'" —NKJV*